Understanding Presidential Elections:
The Constitution, Caucuses, Primaries, The Electoral College, and More

Catherine McGrew Jaime

Other Books by Catherine:

Understand and Teaching the U.S.
    Constitution

The Philadelphia Convention:
    A Play for Many Readers

Failure in Philadelphia?
    (historical fiction)

Understanding the Electoral College

Understanding Caucuses and
    Primaries

Leonardo the Florentine
    (historical fiction)

Leonardo: His Life and His Legacy

Creative Learning Connection
8006 Old Madison Pike, Ste 11-A
Madison, AL 35758
www.CreativeLearningConnection.com

Table of Contents

Introduction

Every four years citizens of the United States go to the ballot box to cast their vote in the election process of their Chief Executive – the President of the United States. But many students and adults alike do not understand the process by which we elect our president. Are we really casting a vote directly for one of them or for an elector, and what is the difference?

And going backwards from November, how did those men and/or women end up on the November ballot in the first place? What is the process of a political party choosing their candidate, through this confusing array of caucuses and primaries that have been held?

This little book will first walk through the constitutional background and basis for this critical office, and then go through the nomination process of caucuses and primaries, ending with the Electoral College process that completes the cycle every four years.

The Constitutional Background

When the colonies declared their independence from Great Britain in 1776 they were not interested in setting up a strong executive; they were in the process of leaving one behind (the King of England).

Under their first constitution, the Articles of Confederation, they formed a league of friendship between the states in an attempt to have the minimum amount of government they thought would help them win the war, and then maintain the peace afterwards. Again, a strong executive was not in their plans.

But by May of 1787 many of them were ready to produce a new constitution to replace the weak Articles of Confederation, and the need for a stronger executive was seen by quite a few of those. But the system we ended up with was by no means the only one they considered, or one that was automatically approved.

From the end of May through September of that year delegates met in Philadelphia to hammer out details of the new Constitution. Agreement was reached fairly quickly that there should be three branches to the new government, but that was one of the only things that was agreed upon quickly.

One of the first items addressed that summer was the Executive branch. Charles Pinckney of South Carolina made it clear immediately that he was for a vigorous

Executive; but that he wanted to ensure they did not make the Executive into a monarchy.

In fact, many times during the debates that summer the need for the avoidance of tyranny came up. Virginia Governor Edmund Randolph made it very clear that he did not think it could ever be appropriate to put the power of the Executive into the hands of one man; three (drawn from different parts of the country) would certainly be better.

Fellow Virginian James Madison quickly pointed out that they might best determine the authority of the executive before they worried about who should comprise the executive. Concern that the chief executive would be given too much power was just as quickly countered by concerns that he be given too little power. Avoiding the appearance of a king was critical to most delegates, but avoiding the chaos they felt under the Articles of Confederation was equally important.

Over the next three months the delegates argued over the manner of election of the chief executive – whether by the states, their elected officials of one sort or another, or horrors of horrors, even by the people directly. (That direct form of democracy had very little popularity.)

There was also the question of term lengths – one, three, and seven years were the most immediate suggestions. Later suggestions of eight and fifteen years were made, at which point, Rufus King of Massachusetts sputtered, "I would prefer twenty years; this is the medium life of princes."

And connected to the issue of term lengths was the question of whether a chief executive should be re-electable or not. Like everything else on the table that summer, that was hotly disputed.

For three months they argued over the important decisions to be made about the executive branch, oftentimes tabling it to debate other important issues like the legislative branch and the judicial branch. But they always returned to the topic of the executive. By mid-August they were often referring to the chief of the executive branch as the President.

By August compromises were being made and the Convention was moving towards enough of a consensus to appoint a committee to draft a final document. (But not before some of the delegates had left in anger over decisions that had already been made.)

By early September a finished document was presented to the convention for the final approval of and signing by the delegates. All of the delegates that remained in Philadelphia at that time signed the document, with the exception of three who had also worked all summer on it – George Mason, Edmund Randolph, and Elbridge Gerry. For a variety of reasons they chose not to put their signatures on the document.

With the convention at an end, the Constitution was sent to the states to ratify. By 1788 enough states (nine) had ratified it for it to become the supreme law of the land, and in the spring of 1789, George Washington was sworn in under it, as the first President of the United States.

The Constitution and the President

Office of the President

After months of debates and compromises, the Philadelphia Convention gave us the Constitution we have today, and with it, most of our ideas of a President.

The second article of the Constitution deals with the office of President, beginning with section one:

> "The executive Power shall be vested in a President of the United States of America. He shall hold his Office during the term of four years, and together with the Vice President, chosen for the same term, be elected as follows..."

The specific details of how to elect the President and Vice President were amended in 1804 by the twelfth amendment.

So right away, the Constitution establishes the Executive branch as having one chief, elected for a four year term, and spells out the process of using electors to choose the president.

The Constitution goes on to give us the minimum age (thirty-five) for a president, along with the citizenship and residence requirements (born a citizen, and residing in the country at least fourteen years).

It even gives us the oath he will take when he is sworn in:

"Before he enter on the Execution of his Office, he shall take the following Oath or Affirmation:--'I do solemnly swear (or affirm) that I will faithfully execute the Office of President of the United States, and will to the best of my Ability, preserve, protect and defend the Constitution of the United States.'"

Section two lists several of the powers of the president, including:

"The President shall be Commander in Chief of the Army and Navy of the United States..."

In 1933, with an improvement in transportation and communication, the 20th Amendment changed the date that the President and Vice President should be sworn in:

> "The terms of the President and the Vice President shall end at noon on the 20th day of January..."

No term limits were set on a President until after World War II, when the 22nd Amendment was ratified in 1951:

> "No person shall be elected to the office of the President more than twice, and no person who has held the office of

President, or acted as President, for more than two years of a term to which some other person was elected President shall be elected to the office of President more than once…"

With that amendment the presidential term limits that some had argued for almost two hundred years earlier had become a part of the Constitution.

Voting For President

The Constitution was initially silent on voting requirements. The first time this was addressed was in 1868 when the 14th Amendment attempted to preclude discrimination against certain voters:

> "But when the right to vote at any election for the choice of electors for President and Vice-President of the United States, Representatives in Congress, the Executive and Judicial officers of a State, or the members of the Legislature thereof, is denied to any of the male inhabitants of such State, being twenty-one years of

age, and citizens of the United States..."

Two years later the Constitution was amended again (the 15th Amendment):

"The right of citizens of the United States to vote shall not be denied or abridged by the United States or by any State on account of race, color, or previous condition of servitude..."

It wasn't until 1920 that the 19th Amendment made it a requirement for women to be given the right to vote (some states were already allowing women to vote, but now they would all be forced to allow it):

"The right of citizens of the United States to vote shall not be denied or abridged by the United States or by any State on account of sex."

And in 1964, in the midst of civil rights violations, the 24th amendment made it clear that poll taxes and other taxes could not be used as an excuse to prevent otherwise eligible voters from voting:

"The right of citizens of the United States to vote in any primary or other election for President or Vice President, for electors for President or Vice President, or for Senator or Representative in Congress, shall not be denied or abridged by the United States or any State by reason of failure to pay poll tax or other tax."

And with the 26th Amendment, in 1971, the voting age was lowered to eighteen:

"The right of citizens of the United States, who are eighteen years of age or older, to vote shall not be denied or abridged by the United States or by any State on account of age."

Understanding Caucuses and Primaries

Convention Delegates: Pledged Vs. Unpledged

There are two types of delegates at the Party Convention, pledged and unpledged (also called bound and unbound in some places).

Most of the delegates have pledged which candidate they will be voting for at the Convention and were chosen at their State's Primary or Caucus for that purpose, but the unpledged can vote for whichever candidate they prefer. Unpledged delegates are also called superdelegates.

Superdelegates include various state and national party leaders who will be able to cast their votes along with those elected delegates.

Where do the pledged delegates come from? That's where Primaries and Caucuses come in. Those begin in January of election year, and continue through June.

Primaries

Primaries are what most of us are familiar with in this stage of the election process. In the states with primaries, voters make their selection by secret ballot on the appointed date in the appointed location.

Generally the ballots list the candidates they may choose from; but in some states the ballots actually list the convention delegates they may choose from.

Closed vs. Open Primaries

Closed primaries are limited to members of that particular party. Any registered voter from that state can vote in an open primary – but if both parties are holding primaries they can only vote in one of them. (And states come up with all sorts of variations on the open or closed concept, from semi-open to semi-closed.)

Party Caucuses

In states that use the Caucus system instead of the Primary system, public meetings are held throughout the state on a specific date at a specific time. Registered voters attend their local meeting and gather in groups based on their preferred candidate. (As opposed to Primaries, a voter has to be present to participate in the caucus; there are no absentee voters in a Caucus situation.)

Caucuses are much more informal than primaries, and do not involve the casting of a physical ballot, instead, at an appointed time the size of each group will be counted, and the numbers will be sent on to the state party where they will be tallied with the results of other

Caucuses statewide. How many delegates each candidate will receive is based on the number of people counted in their group at the individual Caucuses. Candidates with a broader base of organization tend to do better in the caucus states.

The Texas "Two-Step"

And then there's Texas – which, at least until recently, had its own combination of a primary and caucuses. During the day voters voted in a primary; two-thirds of the state's designated delegates were awarded proportionally according to those results.

That evening anyone who voted during the day would have the opportunity to attend a local caucus, where they would again be able to make their choice known. As a result of the caucuses, the remaining third of designated delegates were selected. (Texas also has a large number of superdelegates who vote the way they want when they go to the Party Convention in the summer.)

In 2012 Texas was in the midst of a fight over redistricting from the 2010 census, and was having difficulty even getting a date set for their primary, no longer a problem by the 2016 election.

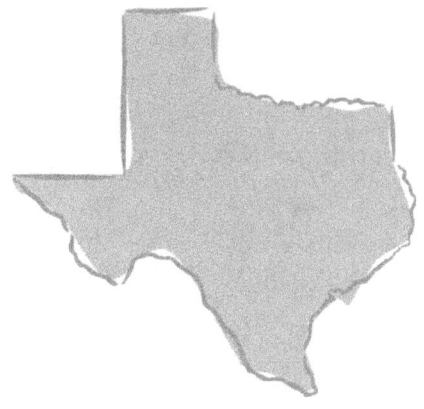

Timing

States set the dates for their primaries and caucuses, but Iowa traditionally starts the caucus trail, traditionally holding their caucuses in early January (though in 2016 they moved back to early February), followed by New Hampshire's primary a week later.

Several more states hold their caucuses and their primaries over the next six weeks, one, two, or three at a time. The first Tuesday in March has been referred to as Super Tuesday, and more than a dozen states hold their caucuses and primaries on that one day, the largest number in a single day.

The Missouri Solution

Missouri ran into a problem of their own in 2012. Their state law required a primary in February, but the Republican Party started penalizing states other than Iowa, New Hampshire, South Carolina, and Nevada, who scheduled primaries or caucuses before Super Tuesday. So Missouri scheduled a non-binding primary for February and a binding caucus date for March.

By the 2016 election, Missouri Republicans had changed to a binding open primary in March and April caucus dates to just choose the actual delegates representing the state at the National Convention. (The Democrats there have just the March open primary.)

Delegate Numbers

States each have a quantity of delegates at their party's convention based on population (based on their congressional districts). When the Democratic Party is holding caucuses and primaries, they award delegates in each states in a proportional basis, according to what the voters had declared that day.

Republicans, on the other hand, award delegates on a proportional basis in some states, but in others on a "winner take all" basis, where the candidate with the most votes take all of that state's delegates at the convention.

At the party convention, a candidate wins their party's nomination when they have at least one more than fifty percent of the delegates. In close races, the decision may come down to the actual convention, but in many elections the outcome is clear before the later states have even held their primaries and caucuses.

2016 Primaries and Caucuses

A list of dates and types of primaries or caucuses that each state has scheduled for the 2016 election cycle is on the next page. Oftentimes the Democrats and Republicans hold them on the same date, if not, there are two dates listed.

2016 Presidential Primaries and Caucuses – By State

State   Form   Date(s):

Alabama
   Open Primary, March 1
Alaska
   Closed Caucuses, March 1 & 26
Arizona
   Closed Primary, March 22
Arkansas
   Open Primary, March 1
California
   Semi-Open Primary, June 7
Colorado
   Closed Caucuses, March 1
Connecticut
   Closed Primary, April 26
Delaware
   Closed Primary, April 26

District of Columbia
   Closed Caucuses/Primaries,
   March 12 & June 14
Florida
   Closed Primary, March 15
Georgia
   Open Primary, March 1
Hawaii
   Closed Caucuses, March 8 & 26
Idaho
   Closed Caucus/Primary,
   March 8 & 22
Illinois
   Open Primary, March 15
Iowa
   Closed Caucuses, Feb 1
Indiana
   Open Primary, May 3
Kansas
   Closed Caucuses, March 5

Kentucky
  Closed Caucus/Primary,
  March 5 & May 17
Louisiana
  Closed Primary, March 5
Maine
  Closed Primary/Caucus,
  March 5 & 6
Maryland
  Closed Primary, April 26
Massachusetts
  Semi-Open Primary, March 1
Michigan
  Open Primary, March 8
Minnesota
  Open Caucus, March 1
Mississippi
  Open Primary, March 8
Missouri
  Open Primary, March 15
Montana
  Open Primary, June 7

Nebraska
  Closed Caucus/Primary,
  March 5 & May 10
Nevada
  Closed Caucuses, Feb 20 & 23
New Hampshire
  Semi-Open Primary, February 9
New Jersey
  Semi-Open Primary, June 7
New Mexico
  Closed Primary, June 7
New York
  Closed Primary, April 19
North Carolina
  Semi-Closed Primary, March 15
North Dakota
  Closed Caucuses, Mar 1 & Jun 7
Ohio
  Semi-Open Primary, March 15
Oklahoma
  Closed Primary, March 1

Oregon
  Closed Primary, May 17
Pennsylvania
  Closed Primary, Apr 26
Rhode Island
  Semi-Open Primary, April 26
South Carolina
  Open Primary, February 20 & 27
South Dakota
  Closed Primary, June 7
Tennessee
  Open Primary, March 1
Texas
  Open Primary, March 1
Utah
  Closed Primary, March 22
Vermont
  Open Primary, March 1
Virginia
  Open Primary, March 1

Washington
  Closed Caucus/Primary,
  March 26 & May 24
West Virginia
  Semi-Open Primary, May 10
Wisconsin
  Open Primary, April 5
Wyoming
  Closed Caucuses,
  March 1 & April 9

2016 Presidential Primaries and Caucuses – By Dates

Date   State   Type

February 1
  Iowa Closed Caucus

February 9
  New Hampshire Semi-Open
    Primary

February 20 & 23
  Nevada Closed Caucuses

February 20 & 27
  South Carolina Open Primary

March 1
  Alabama Open Primary
  Arkansas Open Primary
  Colorado Closed Caucuses
  Georgia Open Primary
  Massachusetts Semi-Open
    Primary
  Minnesota Open Caucus
  Oklahoma Closed Primary

March 1, cont:
    Tennessee Open Primary
    Texas Open Primary
    Vermont Open Primary
    Virginia Open Primary
March 1 & 26
    Alaska Closed Caucuses
March 1 & April 9
    Wyoming Closed Caucuses
March 1 & June 7
    North Dakota Closed Caucuses
March 5
    Kansas Closed Caucuses
    Louisiana Closed Primary
March 5 & 6
    Maine Closed Primary/Caucus
March 5 & May 10
    Nebraska Closed Caucus/Primary
March 5 & May 17
    Kentucky Closed Caucus/Primary
March 8
    Michigan Open Primary

March 8, cont:
  Mississippi Open Primary
March 8 & 22
  Idaho Closed Caucus/Primary
March 8 & 26
  Hawaii Closed Caucuses
March 12 & June 14
  District of Columbia
    Closed Caucus/Primary
March 15
  Florida Closed Primary
  Illinois Open Primary
  Missouri Open Primary
  North Carolina
    Semi-Closed Primary
  Ohio Semi-Open Primary
March 22
  Arizona Closed Primary
  Utah Closed Primary
March 26 & May 24
  Washington
    Closed Caucus/Primary

April 5
  Wisconsin Open Primary
April 19
  New York Closed Primary
April 26
  Connecticut Closed Primary
  Delaware Closed Primary
  Maryland Closed Primar
  Pennsylvania Closed Primary
  Rhode Island Semi-Open Primary
May 3
  Indiana Open Primary
May 10
  West Virginia Semi-Open Primary
May 17
  Oregon Closed Primary
June 7
  California Semi-Open Primary
  Montana Open Primary
  New Jersey Semi-Open Primary
  New Mexico Closed Primary
  South Dakota Closed Primary

Understanding Caucuses and Primaries Activity

As my government students watched the election results week after week and tried to make sense of what was going on, it occurred to me that we needed to have a clearer look at what the difference is between the various ways that states choose their delegates for the national conventions in the summer/fall of each presidential election cycle:

What does proportional representation look like versus "winner take all"? Why are some primaries closed and some open? And where do caucuses fit into all this?

We had already been discussing primaries and caucuses to some degree. But, in order to better demonstrate these to my students, I wanted them to actually walk through some of the differences, just as we had done the year before to see the differences between Democracies and Republics (in my Democracy vs. Republic Mini Lesson).

First, I divided the class into four different groups, each with between five and eight students. (I did not make the groups all the same size, since states are not all the same and each group would be representing a state for the first activity.)

After it was clear who was in which group, we turned our attention to primaries, to see the results of selecting delegates based on winner take all versus proportional. We chose to focus on the four Republican candidates currently vying for the Republican nomination, since they were currently in the news so much, but the exercise could be done with any choice of candidates, real or imaginary, current or historical.

We wrote the four candidates across the top of the white board, to track how many delegates they were winning. (For simplicity's sake, we were using the same number of delegates as there were voters in each of our "states," but I reminded the students that those numbers would not actually be the same in real state elections.)

We counted the total delegates in the room that would be attending our small party convention, and determined what the minimum number (one more than fifty percent) that a candidate would need to win our nomination. (For our simulation we had twenty-eight delegates, so a candidate would need fifteen delegates to win the nomination.)

Each group chose a state that they would represent from a list of states that choose delegates by primaries, so that we could keep the focus on what states are doing in this process. I put each chosen state up on the board along the left side of the board. To simplify things we didn't worry about which states use proportional distribution and which use the "winner take all" method, since we were going to compare the results of each method anyway.

On the first board we awarded the proportionally chosen delegates for each state. On a second board I wrote the candidates and states again. This time we awarded delegates in the "winner take all" fashion. With our particular group, one candidate barely won enough delegates with the proportional distribution, but won it handily when we changed to "winner take all," where he won the delegates from three of the four states.

After our experience with the primaries, I explained that in the next simulation we were one caucus location in a caucus state, and we would pick our delegates with that matter. I chose one student for each candidate to start the grouping in their particular corner. Then I encouraged students to join the group of their preferred candidate.

If they were undecided, they were to go around the room and meet with the groups of the different candidates. The different groups worked at encouraging the undecided voters to join their particular group. After a time of milling and discussing, I had each group count the number of committed voters that had joined their group.

Surprisingly, the number of voters for our previous winner actually went down slightly, and he no longer had a sufficient number of voters to win the fifty percent plus one requirement.

The students returned to their seats and we discussed the different results between the three methods, which ones they liked better, and what the advantages and disadvantages to them were.

We finished the lesson by having each state determine whether they would prefer to hold a caucus or a primary, and whether they would go with a "winner take all" option or a proportional distribution of delegates. In our classroom, all four states chose to have a primary over a caucus. Two chose the "winner take all" and two chose the proportional distribution.

By this time I was quite confident that we had gotten our point across, and that the students now had a better idea of the difference between a caucus and a primary, and many of the nuances that went along with them.

Understanding the Electoral College

What is the Electoral College?

Every four years Americans go to the ballot box and cast their votes for their preference for president, and at least every four years there are complaints and concerns about the process we use to elect our president.

We use something very unique in this country: The Electoral College. The Electoral College is a group of 538 men and women (Electors) from throughout the United States who meet in each state capital and in the nation's capital on one day in December of a presidential election year to formally elect the next president of the United States.

Wait, you may say, we vote for president in November of that year. No, not actually. We vote for the Electors who will vote for president.

The next President of the United States will be the man or woman who receives at least 270 electoral votes (a simple majority – half of the 538 plus one), not the one who receives the largest number of popular votes. Generally the same person wins both, but not always. And it doesn't matter, because we don't elect the President of this country by popular votes.

How do we Pick our Electors to the Electoral College?

Each state has the number of Electors equal to the number of Senators and the number of Representatives they have. So currently each state has at least three electors, and as many as fifty-five. (Before 1961, citizens of the nation's capital had no say in our Presidential elections. Then the 23rd Amendment gave the District of Columbia three electors in the Electoral College, the same number as the lowest populated state.)

In forty-nine of the fifty-one "states" (D.C. is treated as a state for this matter), the electors are chosen in a "winner take all" process. In other words, when the votes for those forty-nine states are counted up on and after Election Day, the candidate with the highest number receives all of that state's electors.

Chickadee

Meadowlark

The last two states, Maine and Nebraska, do not have a winner take all system. In both states, the candidate with the largest number of votes receives two electoral votes immediately (for the senators' portion). The remainder of the votes are associated with each district (for the representatives' portion).

The winner of each district wins that district's electoral vote. So in theory, multiple candidates can win electors from both of those states. (Sadly, this dilutes the influence of both of those states, rather than increasing it.)

Prior to Election Day, each major political party has selected their slate of electors that will vote in December if their party wins that state. When the electors meet across the country to cast their ballots, most are not required by law to vote for the candidate of their party (it depends on the laws in their state). But "faithless electors" are rare; seldom will an Elector stray from the vote he/she is expected to cast.

History of the Electoral College

The process goes back (with some minor tweaking) to the ratification of our Constitution over 200 years ago, and is in the opinion of many (including this author!) one of the most brilliant things our founders accomplished.

Our founders had many options they could have chosen for electing the president. One straightforward way would have been to just have a "popularity contest" and give the office to the man with the most votes nationwide. (They weren't even allowing women to vote at that time, let alone run for office.)

Another way would have been to let the governors of each state cast a vote for the president…Or the House of Representatives could have elected him…And on the options went. They chose none of those. Instead they came up with a system that is not as complicated as it initially appears.

The first thing to remember about this process is that we are not a democracy in this country, we are a **republic**. We have a republican form of government – meaning we vote for representatives, who make decisions for us. Our founding fathers were very conscious of developing a system that would prevent "mob rule" or the "tyranny of the majority."

Another important point is that **states** were important entities in the eyes of the founders. They were not just forming a **national** government (where we were a large nation operating as one). They were also forming a **federal** government which brought together the confederation of states. The States were not going to lose their separate identity and function in the process.

The next thing to remember is that our founders tried to set up a form of government that looked out for the interests of both the **small states** and the **large states**. This was a very real concern during the Constitutional Convention. In fact, it was a concern that almost kept the Constitution from being finished, and from being ratified (accepted by the states) once it was finished.

The founders also had a general mistrust of putting too much power into the hands of everyday citizens. They were very wary of anything that was too "democratic" — believing that it would be too easy for the wants of the majority to trample the needs of the minority in that situation.

All of those concerns led to the system we have come to refer to as the Electoral College.

Federalists and the Electoral College

John Jay

During the ratification process of the Constitution (while the various states debated passing it), Alexander Hamilton, John Jay, and James Madison wrote a number of essays (Federalist Papers) to give their thoughts and arguments in favor of the Constitution.

In Federalist Paper #10, James Madison explained the advantages of a republic over a democracy:

"The two great points of difference between a democracy and a republic are: first, the delegation of the government, in the latter, to a small number of citizens elected by the rest; secondly, the greater number of citizens, and greater sphere of country, over which the latter may be extended."

James Madison

James Madison explained more about the **national** versus **federal** idea towards the end of Federalist Paper #39:

"Were it wholly national, the supreme and ultimate authority would reside in the MAJORITY of the people of the Union; and this authority would be competent at all times…to alter or abolish its established government.

Were it wholly federal, on the other hand, the concurrence of each State in the Union would be essential to every alteration that would be binding on all. The mode provided by the plan of the convention is not founded on either of these principles.

In requiring more than a majority, and particularly in computing the proportion by STATES, not by CITIZENS, it departs from the NATIONAL and advances towards the FEDERAL character; in rendering the concurrence of less than the whole number of States sufficient, it loses again the FEDERAL and partakes of the NATIONAL character."

In this particular place Madison is discussing the method they have chosen to make the Constitution amendable, but his arguments also hold true for the way they set up the Electoral College.

Alexander Hamilton

In Federalist Paper #68 Alexander Hamilton defended the Electoral College they were establishing. He used the word "electors," he didn't use the term "Electoral College" which does not come into common usage until later:

> "And as the electors, chosen in each State, are to assemble and vote in the State in which they are chosen, this detached and divided situation will expose them much less to heats and ferments...

They have not made the appointment of the President to depend on any preexisting bodies of men, who might be tampered with beforehand...the choice of persons for the temporary and sole purpose of making the appointment... Their transient existence and their detached situation, already taken notice of, afford a satisfactory prospect of their continuing so, to the conclusion of it..."

The Advantages of this System

Some would prefer we go to a popularity contest to elect our President, a more democratic thing to do they claim. If we did that, the power of the larger states would be even greater. All a candidate would need would be to win the most populous states and the contest would be over. Voters in small states would have even less influence than they do now.

And again, we are not a democracy. We are a republic. As the Constitutional Convention came to a close, Benjamin Franklin was asked "What have you wrought?" His quick response was: "…A Republic, if you can keep it."

Benjamin Franklin

We don't want to get to a place where the majority of the people in our country can trample over the minority just because they are the majority. (Where are the concerns for "minority rights" in this type of discussion?)

In fact, if we go to a popularity contest, a candidate wouldn't even have to have a majority – all they would need would be a plurality (more than anyone else). If at least three candidates are running, that can be far less than fifty percent!

To become president in our current situation, a candidate must convince **enough** voters in **enough** states that he is the man for the job. Even small states have a say with this system.

Additionally, since popular vote is only considered on a state by state basis, the inherent danger of voter fraud is kept to a minimum. If we went to a popular vote, massive voter fraud in just a few places could affect the outcome of the election.

The "Disadvantages"
of this System

Someone can be the most popular candidate and still not win the election. This has only happened a handful of times in the more than fifty presidential elections we've held in this country (including 1824, 1876, 1888).

In each of those cases the "popular winner" did not win the Electoral College votes because they were not popular in enough states. In other words, they did not have the wide geographical support necessary.

Can the System be Changed?

Only by a constitutional amendment. This is the most frequently suggested amendment to our constitution – over 500 such amendments have been suggested in the past. Fortunately our founders made it difficult to amend the United States Constitution, and so far no one has succeeded in changing this.

The only other changes that can be made to the system are the way individual states divvy up their electoral votes. (Since the specifics of that is not mandated by the Constitution.)

Colorado tried that in 2004. They were not successful. It was understood by the majority of the voters in Colorado that changing their system would lessen their importance in the Presidential election, not increase it. (With the suggested change, a candidate would have been most likely to win four or five electoral votes from Colorado, rather than zero or nine!)

Columbine

Conclusion

As we get closer to the next Presidential Election, may we think more highly of the Founders who worked so hard to give us an electoral system that has served us well for over 200 years!

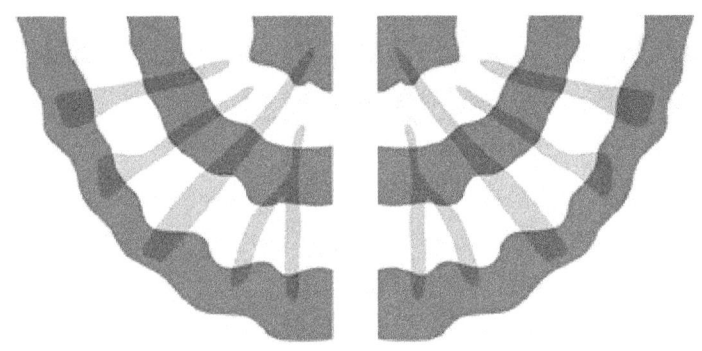

For More Information

There is a great Disney movie (The One and Only, Original Family Band) that deals with the electoral votes versus the popular vote from the 1888 election where Grover Cleveland won the popular votes, but Benjamin Harrison won the election with the largest number of electoral votes.

Grover Cleveland

Benjamin Harrison

My favorite line from the movie is when the disappointed grandfather complains, "What's some college got to do with it anyway?"

Aristoplay Game: Hail to the Chief : They say it well on their website www.aristoplay.com "Players move around the outside of the board answering questions on presidents and the Constitution, as you become a candidate...Learn how the election process works as well as fascinating historical and geographical facts."

Website Resources

I found the following websites to be useful in my search to understand the Electoral College:

Does my vote count? Teaching the Electoral College by David Walbert: www.learnnc.org/lp/media/lessons/ davidwalbert7232004-02/ electoralcollege.html

National Archives site with answers to Frequently Asked Questions about the Electoral College: www.archives.gov/federal-register/ electoral-college/faq.html

Great article about the attempt to pass Amendment 36 in Colorado: www.freecolorado.com/ 2004/10/36qa.html

Any of the Federalist Papers can be read in their entirety on this website:

http://www.yale.edu/lawweb/avalon/federal/fed.htm

Electoral Votes for the District of Columbia and Each State, Numerical Order

(as of the 2010 census)

State	Votes
District of Columbia	3
Alaska	3
Delaware	3
Montana	3
North Dakota	3
South Dakota	3
Vermont	3
Wyoming	3
Hawaii	4
Idaho	4
Maine	4

New Hampshire	4
Rhode Island	4
Nebraska	5
New Mexico	5
West Virginia	5
Arkansas	6
Iowa	6
Kansas	6
Mississippi	6
Nevada	6
Utah	6
Connecticut	7
Oklahoma	7
Oregon	7
Kentucky	8
Louisiana	8

Alabama	9
Colorado	9
South Carolina	9
Maryland	10
Minnesota	10
Missouri	10
Wisconsin	10
Arizona	11
Indiana	11
Massachusetts	11
Tennessee	11
Washington	12
Virginia	13
New Jersey	14
North Carolina	15
Georgia	16

Michigan	16
Ohio	18
Illinois	20
Pennsylvania	20
Florida	29
New York	29
Texas	38
California	55
Total	**538**

Electoral Votes
Alphabetically
(as of the 2010 census)

State	Votes
Alabama	9
Alaska	3
Arizona	11
Arkansas	6
California	55
Colorado	9
Connecticut	7
Delaware	3
District of Columbia	3
Florida	29
Georgia	16
Hawaii	4

Idaho	4
Illinois	20
Indiana	11
Iowa	6
Kansas	6
Kentucky	8
Louisiana	8
Maine	4
Maryland	10
Massachusetts	11
Michigan	16
Minnesota	10
Mississippi	6
Missouri	10
Montana	3
Nebraska	5

Nevada	6
New Hampshire	4
New Jersey	14
New Mexico	5
New York	29
North Carolina	15
North Dakota	3
Ohio	18
Oklahoma	7
Oregon	7
Pennsylvania	20
Rhode Island	4
South Carolina	9
South Dakota	3
Tennessee	11
Texas	38

Utah	6
Vermont	3
Virginia	13
Washington	12
West Virginia	5
Wisconsin	10
Wyoming	3
Total	**538**

About the Author

Catherine Jaime is the co-author of an article on the Electoral College in a national publication on the American Government. She has also authored several books dealing with government and economics.

Catherine firmly believes in the importance of the U.S. Constitution and the free market, and it shows in her writings.

Catherine has been teaching high school economics and

government for almost twenty years. She loves sharing her passion for these subjects with her students and her readers.

Catherine did her under-graduate work at the Sloan School of Management at the Massachusetts Institute of Technology, in Cambridge, Massachusetts, and has continued her economics training through the Foundation for Teaching Economics and the Foundation for Economic Education.

Catherine can be reached at cmmjaime@alum.mit.edu,

and more of her books (on this topic and many others!) can be found on her website, www.CatherineJaime.com as well as on many major book retailer sites.

As an indie author, Catherine would be thrilled if you would do her the honor of a review upon completion of her book.

www.ingramcontent.com/pod-product-compliance
Lightning Source LLC
Chambersburg PA
CBHW071326310526
45789CB00016B/934